TWICE ALIVE

AN ECOLOGY OF INTIMACIES

ALSO BY FORREST GANDER
FROM NEW DIRECTIONS

POETRY
Be With
Core Samples from the World
Eiko & Koma
Eye Against Eye
Science and Steepleflower
Torn Awake

FICTION
As a Friend
The Trace

TRANSLATIONS
Firefly under the Tongue by Coral Bracho
It Must Be a Misunderstanding by Coral Bracho
The Galloping Hour by Alejandra Pizarnik

AS EDITOR
Alice Iris Red Horse by Gozo Yoshimasu

TWICE ALIVE
AN ECOLOGY OF INTIMACIES

Forrest Gander

 A New Directions Book

Manufactured in the United States of America
First published in 2021 as New Directions Paperbook 1498
Design by Arlene Goldberg

Library of Congress Cataloging-in-Publication Data
Names: Gander, Forrest, 1956– author.
Title: Twice alive / Forrest Gander.
Description: New York, NY : New Directions Books, 2021.
Identifiers: LCCN 2020054953 | ISBN 9780811230292 (paperback)
Subjects: LCGFT: Poetry.
Classification: LCC PS3557.A47 T85 2021 | DDC 811/.54—dc23
LC record available at https://lccn.loc.gov/2020054953

10 9 8 7 6 5 4 3 2

New Directions Books are published for James Laughlin
by New Directions Publishing Corporation
80 Eighth Avenue, New York 10011

For Ashwini Bhat & Lakshmi Bhat

a garden without lichens / is a garden without hope
—*Drew Milne*

My every moment / I've lived / a second time . . .
—*Giuseppe Ungaretti*
(Geoffrey Brock, trans.)

Who need be afraid of the merge?
—*Walt Whitman*

CONTENTS

Author's note   9

Aubade   13
Unto Ourselves   14
Twice Alive   17
Sangam Acoustics
    Forest   21
    Immigrant Sea   24
    In the Mountains   26
    Pastoral   28
    Wasteland (for Santa Rosa)   30
Aubade II   33
Unto Ourselves II: The Persistence of Dispersed Worlds   34
Twice Alive II: Tahoe National Forest   38
Sangam Acoustics II
    Post-fire Forest   41
    Sea: Night Surfing in Bolinas   42
    In the Mountains, Placer County   44
    Pastoral   46
    Wasteland   48
Aubade III   51
Unto Ourselves III: To See What's There   52
Twice Alive III: Circumabulation of Mt. Tamalpais   55
The Redwoods   63
Rexroth's Cabin   72
"Sangam Acoustics: Confluence of Time, Space,
    and the Human Self" by N. Manu Chakravarthy 75

Acknowledgments   81

AUTHOR'S NOTE

What many of us learned in high school about lichen—that it's an indicator species for pollution (litmus, in fact, is derived from lichens), and that it's the synergistic alliance of a fungus and algae or cyanobacteria—is largely true, but simplified. If lichen ecology has more to do with collaboration than competition, it's nevertheless true that collaboration is transformative. With lichen, which may be more related to animals than plants, the original organisms are changed utterly in their compact. They can't return to what they were. And according to Anne Pringle, one of the leading contemporary mycologists (with whom I had the lucky opportunity to collaborate), it may be that lichen do not, given sufficient nutrients, age. Anne and other contemporary biologists are saying that our sense of the inevitability of death may be determined by our mammalian orientation. Perhaps some forms of life have "theoretical immortality." Lichens can reproduce asexually, and when they do, bits of both partners are dispersed together to establish in a new habitat. How long can the partners of a lineage continue to reproduce? No one knows. The thought of two things that merge, mutually altering each other, two things that, intermingled and interactive, become one thing that does not age, brings me to think of the nature of intimacy. Isn't it often in our most intimate relations that we come to realize that our identity, all identity, is combinatory?

TWICE ALIVE

AN ECOLOGY OF INTIMACIES

AUBADE

Can you hear dawn edging close, hear • soft light with its vacuum

fingertips • gripping the bedroom wall, an understated • what?

exhilaration? Can you hear the voices, • if they can be called voices,

of towhees • scratching in the garden and then • the creaky low

husky • voice flecked with sleep beside you in bed • telling a dream

slowly as though in real time, • and now, interrupting that dream,

can you • make out the voice, if it can be • called a voice, of

absence speaking • intimately to you, directly, I know • you must

hear it feelingly, a low vibration in • your bones, for don't you find

yourself • absorbed in a next moment beyond your given life?

Even when we realized we'd stopped, in every
essential way stopped moving forward, when
we came to see we were descending, even
more tightly bound to the vortex
as images rushed by in front of us and a blue
whale rotted on the sand in Bolinas, its stink
drifting southward where dozens of barnacled
forty-foot grays, dead from starvation, began to hulk
against the shore, the white-tufted foreheads
of waves smashing against those
knolls of oily decomposing flesh, it was
everywhere we looked if we cared to look
out over bitesize squares of cheese
and Saintsbury wine into the hum
taking place under a coved moon, or cared to
listen to clumped wild-rye
shushing the dunes
while pulverized rock shrieked along fault lines
in decibels so muted only the soles of our feet,
conducting the ground's sound
up into our tali, could register what
was happening
right there where our lives had been
cut off from themselves and become something else
drained of substance, steeped in the privilege
against which we protested with those we called
our friends—the ones who lately seemed
to contract backward from our greetings,
giving us to suspect
that they too sensed something askew, the

skip at the center of ourselves or just an
inkling of abyssal unhappiness was it? concentrated
into the early evenings
like one of those spectral white
fallow deer introduced to the headlands
that began to outcompete
native species and so,
before they were slaughtered every one
by hired hunters, inciting
arguments about what was native if
all systems are given to change. Maybe
our ear twitches. Maybe the deer's ear
twitches. But we still can't quite
make out in the dimness
what we're looking at, can we?
Nor is there interim from the tumult of in-
coming, the masticating chores, ping-
pings begging immediate response, the sheer
overabundance of the present
shame which plugs up each minute and
stands in now for whatever it meant
to live oneself before every gesture
became performance for an audience
we imagine never to be finished
with looking at us. And as for the budding-out
of being we'd called passion? or the sensual
moments phrased into our gait
when we were coming to feel something,
when our shadows merged (not as
romance, but the real consequence

of our mutuality) with
shadows of conifers 'along the steep
ravine, and completely naked and
without relief, the world parsed us
into the inhuman where rosette
lichen surged across rocks lacking nothing
that might be needed to answer
for our existence?
By now, some of us,
outmaneuvered by the economy,
were lying around Dolores Park like fallen fruit
waiting to rot. Others found themselves
receptive to a trivial, self-justifying kindness.
What with coral belching up its algae, evaporating
stars, the waking tundra, how could we bear, we
wondered to each other, even the weight of
our own sorry initiatives? *Life,* someone
countered, *is pure gratuitous magnitude. Just
look: the light is there, grace itself.* But
it was already noon and as we looked,
the colors of the hills began to blanch,
and all around us, in the field of the visible,
we sensed, without speaking, duration's ebb.

TWICE ALIVE

mycobiont just beginning to **en-
wrap** photobiont, each to become
something else, its own life and a
contested mutuality, twice alive,
algal cells **swaddled** in clusters

you take a 3-lens jeweler's loupe to inspect the **holdfast**
of the umbilicate lichens then the rock-tripe lichens
then the irenic Amanita mushroom
swarming with a kind of mite that has no anus
then the delicious chanterelles called Trumpets of Death

supreme parsimony in drought
lets lichen live on
sporadic events
of dew and fog, a **velvety**
tomentum and the wet thallus

I crush oak moss between finger and thumb
for its sweet **perfume** persistent on
your skin when I touch your throat, so slow
to evaporate, the memory of seeing
sunburst lichen on the sandstone cliff

though crustose lichen relish
decay, **vagrant** lichen go all
hygroscopic, spores spurting
out through walls **split**
at the invagination fronts

but if herbivores eat **wolf** lichen they
die and if carnivores eat it they die
writhing in pain with the exception of mice
it is rarely possible to tell
if lichen is dead or alive

the fuzz of **fecal** dust from
lichenivorous mites
triggers woodcutter's eczema,
the bane of loggers knee-deep
in **sweet** fern sawing down cedar

in the presence of water, photobionts go turgid
in hours of dark respiration, a spermatic **green-corn** smell
takes the shape of a lamellated mushroom
in cavitating symplasts, spores loosen
into the **elongation** zone on a night of caterwauling loons

so evening finds us at this woods' edge where
at a dead oak's base
shoestring-rot **glimmers,** its luminescent
rhizomes reflected from the eyes
of a foraging raccoon that doesn't yet sense us

air ghostly and damp clings
as we step from our woods
to look across the field toward the first
lane of lit houses, their dull **pewter**
auras restrained by wet haze

cordyceps—the brown of your eyes softened
with rain and remotely **fluorescent**—dissolve
into **slime** after a few days, whatever we thought
we were following was following us, its
intention unlinked to our own

SANGAM ACOUSTICS

FOREST

Erogenous zones in oaks
        slung with
                stoles of lace lichen the

sun's rays spilling
        through leaves in
                broken packets a force

call it nighttime
        thrusts mushrooms up
                from their lair

of spawn mycelial
        loam the whiff of port
                they pop into un-

trammeled air with the sort of
        gasp that follows
                a fine chess move

like memories are they? or punctuation? was it
        something the earth said
                to provoke our response

tasking us to recall
        an evolutionary
                course our long ago

initiation into
        the one-
           among-others

and within
        my newborn noticing have you
                popped up beside me love

or were you here from the start
        a swarm of meaning and decay
                still gripping the underworld

both of us half-buried holding fast
        if briefly to a swelling
                vastness while our coupling begins

to register in the already
        awake compendium that offers
                to take us in you take me in

and abundance floods us floats
              us out we fill each
                            with the other all morning

breaks as birdsong over us
              who rise to the surface
                            so our faces might be sprung

IMMIGRANT SEA

Aroused by her inaccessibility, he aches for more
of her life to live inside him. Watching

                    the breakers, standing so close he can feel
                      heat coming off her wet scalp. What is

his relation to this person
before him, so familiar and foreign? The way

            he searches out her face, he searches out himself. Gusts
                thrash crests of swell, spring grasses twirl

circles in the sand where they stand without speaking. She
wants him to know it's all charged, even grass

                positive, pollen negative, so when grass waves,
            it sweeps the air for pollen. He feels electricity all around

as though the wild drama of the coming storm were already
aware of them, foreigners on this shore. Little

                sapphire-blue flowers speckle the dunes.
            He wonders if he has let himself flatten out

into a depthless sheet, like escalator stairs, whether in the end
he'll disappear underground without the smallest lurch

of resistance. But when her lavish face turns toward him
beaming, the corners of her eyes wind-wet,

he yields to that excess, he reappears to himself.

IN THE MOUNTAINS

*"No hay exterior del cuerpo. O mejor dicho,
el exterior ocurre dentro del cuerpo"*
—Juan Sebastián Cárdenas

If the April dog days reach her before your note does

If at your back door, a mushroom speckled with roving mites
turns the color of rodent teeth

Then her thighs will tremble, her head go light as she tries to stand

If her irises flare, if your collied face stares back from her pupils dull
   as a writ

Then you must acknowledge the presentiment that you've been
   cored

If you take another sip of dust, trying to remember what to say

If the sludge she calls your sadness stops damming-up your veins

Could she glimpse what was there before you turned inside yourself?

If the regrets edge up behind you chattering

Then she will blindfold you saying: taste this

If it takes just one more crossed-out name to complete the bitterness

If ululations rising from the hills are answered in her face

Then whatever you gasp while she lies over you will sound like
  nonsense from a play

If you reflexively choose the first response that precludes thinking

Then she will cry out *Oh no* as though surprised she can't stop it

If the Western Ghats swallow a carbonized sun

If she mistakes that tic at your eye's crease for a signal

If when she sets her basket on the counter, the ripest mango topples
  from the peak

You must forget the other hands that have opened her robe

If local animals make themselves nocturnal to avoid you, if swarms
  of laughing thrushes no longer descend from the summit

Then the barest gleam from her eyes in the night will reel you in

But if this orange lichen—gossiping across boulders—blackens,
  curls, and goes silent?

PASTORAL

The rain broke off   an hour earlier, the turn
the turn-signal indicator ceased   the last of its clucking, and

we arrived   at the abandoned farm arrived
with others just now   bailing themselves out

from their cars, our voices   pitched in some ad-
mixture of ease and   exhilaration, some

adventure in happiness if   there were such a thing and it wasn't
pretend: laughing, slamming   the doors, we were miscible, we believed

we were friends, remember that?   and your floriferous
bridesmaids still wearing those   purple plumeria headbands

like Goa hippies. The serpentine   footpath to the river steamed—
it steamed in sunlight   adding to the fullness without

adding weight. You,   to whom this place was a given,
sacred even, and so not given   *to* you, pointed out

peacock tracks in the mud. Through   an old orchard on either side
of us, where swollen jackfruit   hung on slender limbs,

swarms of midges   bobbed up and down
like balled hairnets in the light   breeze. Before it

became visible, we heard   the river *river*
and behind it the   gurgling of runoff

down bluffs of packed alluvium.   Jacaranda perfume
mixed with pong   from your neighbor's

breeder-houses. Who could look   into that afternoon and see
it closing? Our whole   queue halted when you went

to one knee, when you crouched   at a puddle to coo
to a fat toad. Gone   quiet, we were hypnotized

by the signature   enthusiasm
in your face. As the sun   cleared the clouds, you

glanced back to find my eyes   eyes fixed on you, and what
I felt then   gave me cause

to recall   the pleasure breaking out
on the faces of musicians   in that pause

between their last note between   their last note and
the applause. What   you said, what I said. What

we did we did until there was no interval between us.

WASTELAND (FOR SANTA ROSA)

Green spring grass on
       the hills had cured
              by June and by July

                              gone wooly and
                        brown, it crackled
              underfoot, desiccated while

within the clamor of live
          oaks, an infestation of
               tiny larvae clung

                        to the underleaves,
                    feeding between
             veins. Their frass, that

fine dandruff of excrement
          and boring dust, tinkled
                  as it dropped onto dead leaves

below the limbs. You
could hear it twenty
feet away, tinkling.

Across the valley, on
Sugarloaf Ridge, the full
moon showed up

like a girl doing cartwheels.
No one goes on living
the life that isn't there.

Below a vast column of
smoke, heat, flame, and
wind, I rose, swaying

and tottering on my
erratic vortex, extemporizing
my own extreme weather, sucking up

acres of scorched
     topsoil and spinning it
          outward in a burning sleet

               of filth and embers that
          catapulted me forward
        with my mouth open

in every direction at once. So
       I came for you, churning, turning
           the present into purgatory

               because I need to turn
          everything to tragedy before
       I can see it, because

it must be
     leavened with remorse
          for the feeling to rise.

AUBADE II
for Ötzi

Pulling the arrow's shaft • from his own shoulder • on the east

ridge with • and an axe of solid copper and • ibex meat undi-

gested • conifer pollen, so late spring • bearskin snowshoes • a

pouch with his firelighting kit • flint flakes and a tinder conk • the

mushroom kindling an ember for hours • after he turned onto

his stomach • froze & thawed & froze again • for 5,000 years •

what beyond pain • did he hear as the light flickered • flickered

on the mountain's face • what entered his body through the ears •

through the desolate desolated desolation of his eyes • what did he

take • for which he had no name

UNTO OURSELVES II:
THE PERSISTENCE OF DISPERSED WORLDS

Firs trembled at the edge of a massive debris flow

in the asphalt-heat of summer

just between you and me, said the field guide

in an undertone leaning forward, you have to

get beyond the expectation that you're

ever going to pull things together

it was a queer thing to say in a queer time

we use a gender-neutral pronoun we said

to which she answered Whoever

thought anyone was just one thing?

when we got back my friends were jumpy

Did you see the quindes?

Did you see the tucusitos?

The picaflores, the chupamirtos—are they over there?

Across the wall?

What of the huichichiquis?

Don't tell me you blinked as it hovered face to your face

fanning you with the mill of its wings, the guide said

no b.s. did you see the huitzillo?

we admitted we'd witnessed the chuparosa in Petaluma

a large blue-throated one up from Mexico

but the tzunún fled too soon

as if it knew what we would do to its garden

where sheathed filaments of cyanobacteria

wakened by winter rains were serpentining through the soil

leaving long sticky trails through the evening

while we stood on our porch and admired

the soft edges of things in moonlight as though

we were in a Gerhard Richter painting or some seductive

image from an advertising campaign

developing in a bath of chemicals

how to recover the play of life itself yes

the yes of course yes we now yes!

we tried walking in someone else's shoes

but fuck that really it was a sham,

like frogs HAZMAT trucks were beeping as they

reached their destination down the block

though who could take notice

with their eyes glued to the new pilot

the reporter didn't say *fire tomato* he said

fire tornado the abyss with one eye

was there only inconsequential difference

between *I contain multitudes* and *be sure*

to like us or those other hortatory sops

we told each other to make the unbearable bearable?

our extrafloral nectaries were still attracting insects

despite we'd sprayed them with Roundup

the spidery bass player kept to his corner of the stage

as one world is bound to another by silence

and catfacing always infects the blossom-side

in the middle of the argument we noticed

we confront each other like two regions of warped space

swallowing the gravitational screams

emitted from our merging holes

and though we admit to a certain amount of preening and swanking

each assumes our own is the meat-forward dish

You're kidding, I overheard the guide say, really? That's

what you did with your life? So

the lonely night was adjourned like a can of green paint

splashed onto the dining car's windows as we watched

lengths of border wall rush past and go by

the conductor's recorded voice said Make use of thy salt hours

for already thou art deep within the affliction

if that's a mass of black jelly fungi
on the rotting pine branch, if that's a thumb-long
translucent egg sac **pulsating** behind the termite queen
if the rising sun through the blinds wakes us together or
will tomorrow, if **witch's butter** could learn to speak

long soft sarongs of **moss**
ensorcel rocks treestumps up-
lifts of granite and gneiss
pine needles blackberry brambles
arching up wet and **tousled**

as we descend a scrub hillside
our breath visible in flighty morning
air, we enter the forest of quaking
aspen, **spongy** ground
on either side of the path riffled
by creamy edible morels and

poisonous **false** morels, song
of moss under our breath, before you left
you said *Don't be so rational, electronics*
are rational and I wondered what change
I might make that my next words **not** be so

then your telegram of tiny black mosquitoes kept me awake
all night on the porch I could hear big **moths**
before I saw them, when finally I laid down in the huge space
your **absence** left me, the cat pawed my chest
while your towel with its sour smell muffled my face

while I'm dogged through the day by quick sniffs of
sickness, the **sorghum**-thick snot insists
I too am a fleshy protuberance risen momently
from some tangled mycelium so the dead also
speak when I speak **oh** holy holy communion

then the getting **tired** happened
then the white-flecked brown pigeon
flattened itself into the sand, some force
expresses us before we can name it
fragrance **whelms** from incense-cedars

SANGAM ACOUSTICS II

POST-FIRE FOREST

Shadows of shadows without canopy,
phalanxes of carbonized trunks and
snags, their inner momentum shorted-out.
They surround us in early morning
like plutonic pillars, like mute clairvoyants
leading a Sursum Corda, like the excrescence
of some long slaughter. All that moves
is mist lifting, too indistinct to be called
ghostly, from scorched filamental
layers of rain-moistened earth. What
remains of the forest takes place
in the exclamatory mode. Cindered
utterances in a tongue from which
everything trivial has been volatilized,
everything trivial to fire. In a notch,
between near hills stubbled
with black paroxysm, we spin
a familiar sun, liquid glass globed
at the blowpipe's tip. If this landscape
is dreaming, it must dream itself awake.

You have, everyone notes, a rare talent
for happiness. I wonder how
to value that, walking through wreckage.
On the second day, a black-backed
woodpecker answers your call, but we
search until twilight without finding it.

SEA: NIGHT SURFING IN BOLINAS

Maybe enough light • to score a wave • reflecting moonlight, sand
• reflecting moonlight and you • spotting from shore • what you
see only • as silhouette against detonating bands • of blue-white
effervescence • when the crown of the falling • swell explodes
upward • as the underwave blows through it • a flash of visibility
quickly • snuffed by night • the surf fizzling and churning • re-
mitting itself to darkness • with a violent stertor • in competition
with no other sounds

paddling through dicey backwash • the break zone of • waist-high
NW swell • as into a wall of obsidian • indistinguishable from
night sky • diving under, paddling fast • and before I sit • one
arm over my board • I duck and • listen a moment underwater
• to the alien soundscape • not daytime's clicks and whines of •
ship engines and sonar • but a low-spectrum hum • the acoustic
signature of fish, squid, • crustaceans rising en masse • to feed at
the surface I feel • an eerie peacefulness veined with fear

after twenty minutes the eyes • adjust, behind the hand dragging

through water • bioluminescent trails • not enough light • to spot

boils • or flaws in nearing • waves appear even larger • closing-in

fast • then five short strokes into a dimensionless • peeler, two

S-shaped turns, the • kick out, and from shore • your shout

it is cowardice that turns my eyes • from the now-empty beach •

for with you I became • aware of an exceptional chance • I don't

believe in • objective description, only • this mess, experience, the

perceived • world sometimes shared • in which life doesn't • en-

dure, only • the void endures • but your vitality stirred it • leaving

trails of excitation • I've risen from the bottom of • myself to find

ı I exist in you • exist in me and • against odds I've known even

rapture, • rare event, • which calls for • but one witness

IN THE MOUNTAINS, PLACER COUNTY

… whose blunt finger, its hornblende-nail clipped,
circles (so lightly across the crevice knob)

And her green delight of serpentine
laughter (as their tram swoops) over the trunk valley

Car door slammed behind her, she faces the cirque
in denim cutoffs (risen to her pudendum)

And sees no gap in the pleasures nestled
in his eyes watching (her eyes watching)

Above the mission of his face, they swing like
church bells (for mass always sways outward)

A taste of jaggery and warm pennies (oh no,
oh no!) in a wet score grooved by glacial erratics

Where, he asks, as she initiates the uplift, and when
did you learn to do that? (decamping downslope)

A rattler riding its coil (her torso on her hips), she leaves
chatter marks on a succession of moraines

(Dark paired suns) the aureoles dilate
as suction-eddies whirligig along the melt stream

When the supplicant slowly bends, long
thighs separate along the joint plane

No undertow of doubt, every part willing, the forest
encroaches ashen earth (when her knees begin to jerk)

Together,
you
standing
before me before
the picture
window, my arms
around you, our
eyes pitched
beyond our
reflections into—

("into" I'd
written, as
though *there*
swung at the end
of a tunnel,
a passage dotted
with endless
points of
arrival, as
though our gaze
started just outside
our faces and
corkscrewed its way
toward the horizon,
processual,
as if looking
took time to happen
and weren't
instantaneous,

offered whole in
one gesture
before we
ask, before our
will, as if the far
Sonoma mountains
weren't equally ready
to be beheld as
the dead
fly on the sill)—

the distance, a
broad hill of
bright mustard flowers
the morning light
coaxes open.

WASTELAND

You will forever regret the petty-righteous cruelties
you acted out on her,

        the neem tree without blossoms, the twig girdler,
        the burying

beetle, a yellow-and-black apple borer with
its disgusting stench

        which decimated the garden while you were
        distracted. Right

when she was leading you out of something.
A laceration inside a laceration

        into which you tugged her back each night
        until nothing was left

between you but a fear of aging and
your unwearying

        self-concern. That night, the last night
        before

your so-called return, she sent
you a note.

Baby, I miss you, imagine

you're sitting in your leather swivel chair

with your silk boxers on, I'll lift my dress a little

and sit on you (you won't have trouble

sliding into me), my back to you, your hands

inside my sleeves

Look up and the horizon line has gone

                 red as a transparent artery while below you

an alligator-lizard continues to

             slide down the warm ash of the

Long Valley Caldera to dig out

                her nest in toxic fumes. The years

of your footsteps have chewed

                a worn path into lichen spotting

tuff around the rim. You've lost

                    your cadence. No one needs

to tell you that. Her absence

                    goes through and through

you like a winze through

                    crumbling bedrock. No-

thing remains in session

                    but the congress of ants.

AUBADE III

We were servicing the pools of the wealthy • we were opening the
passenger door for the dog • the dog who waits in the truck • dog
staring at the restaurant entrance • so when we come out again
with a napkin • wrapped around a chunk of burrito • whimpers
with excitement • and we don't • feel entirely alone • though it's
true • Yo, la peor de todas • at Arion the printers • were dampen-
ing linen • so the type would cast a shadow • before they tossed
slugs of type • back into the hellbox • in the evening • we tried
to cure a phantom • limb with a mirror • but what is missing • is
inside us. A few were • throwing gang signs and smoking Reggie
• before we boarded at pre-dawn • to sit forever on the runway •
sucking up the spent fuel • of the plane before us • the overhead
ducts spewing noxious air • reflected in the dark window • our
own eyes looking back • looking blank • while neutrinos sleet
through us

To see what's there and not already
patterned by familiarity—for an unpredicted
whole is there, casting a pair of shadows, manipulating
its material, advancing, assembling enough
kinship that we call it *life,* our life, what
is already many lives, the dimensions of
its magnitude veiled to us as we live it—

Across the cytoplasm of adjacent cells
goes a signal that turns you toward me, turns
me into you. We are coupled in quiet
tumult, convergent arguments, an alien
rhythm becoming familiar. A rhythm
of *I am here, never to be peeled away.*
We are become one thing
                                        listening

for what's there and not. Through the storm,
neem trees on the hill stamp wildly
in their roots. We have passed through
the spring, but what thing has passed
through us? Now your laughter
transparentizes me. And whose sense
of the self doesn't swerve? Your unconditional
foreignness grows conditional, stops
being foreign at all. With your nearness,
my lens on the world shifts. A peristaltic
contraction courses through us as a single

wave. No longer can we keep our distance.
Our lips brush, or the tips of ourselves.

But what language are you whispering to me,
your teeth stained by Nilgiri tea, above the trills
and whistles in the high limbs, above the screech
of a bulldozer blade shoving rubble
up the wounded street, above the silence
of an eyeless tick climbing a grass stem? I understand
nothing but the lust your voice incites, the
declamatory tenderness. How, and who can say
what force has cued up this hour for our
small voices to merge into a carnality
that did not exist before now?

Having come to this unforeseen
conjunction, we slip
into one another, we take hold
in a pulse of heat, in a yes and no,
for already we can see
we are no longer what we were

as I find you within me—not fused, not
bonded, but nested. And for you, is it
the same?—the intensity of such
investment, each of us excited
by the volatility of the other which

propels us in a rush as something—
perhaps our lips brush or
the tips of ourselves—strips
away what?—what was before? Was there
even anything before?

The reconfiguration is instantaneous
experience. It is *being*
itself. But whose being now? Was I
endowed with some special pliability so
that becoming part of you I didn't pass
through my own nihilation? And what
does the death of who-you-were mean to me
except that now you are present, constantly.

Because excess is what it took
for us to transform, to effulge. You cast
your life beyond itself. Can't you sense me
within your ecstatic openness
like rain mingling with red earth?
Without you I survived and with you
I live again in a radical augmentation
of identity because we have
effaced our outer limits, because
we summoned each other. In you,
I cast my life beyond itself.

TWICE ALIVE III:
CIRCUMAMBULATION OF MT. TAMALPAIS

maculas of light fallen weightless from
pores in the canopy our senses
part of the **wheeling** life around us and through
an undergrowth stoked with **the unseen**
go the reverberations of our steps

as we hike upward mist holds
the **butterscotch** taste of Jeffrey pine
to the air until we reach a serpentine
barren, **redbud** lilac and open sky, a crust
of frost on low-lying clumps of manzanita

at Redwood Creek, two
tandem runners cross
a wooden bridge over
the stream ahead of us the raspy
check check check of a **scrub jay**

hewing to the Dipsea path while
a plane's slow groan diminishes bayward,
my sweat-wet shirt going cool
around my torso as another runner
goes by, his **cocked** arms held too high

Cardiac Hill's granite boulders appear
freshly sheared Look, you say,
I can see the Farallon Islands there
to the south over those long-backed hills
one behind another a crow **honks**

the moon still up over Douglas
firs on the climb to Rock Spring yellow-
jackets and Painted Lady butterflies
settle on the path where some under-
ground trickle moistens the soil

I predict you'll keep to the shade of
the laurels to **nibble** your
three-anchovy-slices-over-cheese
sandwich while I sprawl on a boulder
in full **sun** sucking a pear

the frass of caterpillars tinkles onto beds of dry
leaves under the oak where a hawk **alights**
with its retinue of **raging** crows we are prey to the ache
of not knowing what will be revealed as
the world lunges forward to introduce itself

clusters of tiny green dots, **bitter** oyster,
line the black stick held in your hand, weak
trees leaning into us as if we were part
of the **wet dark** that sustains their roots
under dead leaves and that Armillaria

since honey mushrooms suck from
the soil chemicals that trigger a tree's
defences, they leech the tree's sap
undetected all the while secreting toxins
to stave off competing species

but in the inseparable
genetic **mosaic** of their thin
root filaments the identity
of any singular species blurs among inter-
active populations, **twice** alive

near the summit, a gleaming
slickenside outcrop
sanctifies the path winding
through a precinct of **greenschists**
whose **lethal** minerals sterilize the ground

the hum of some large insect
Immelmanning around
our heads calls to mind,
you tell me, the **low drone**
of a Buddhist chant

but now we really hear chanting
we can't decode—*Don't
be so rational*—a congregate speech
from the **redtrembling** sprigs, a
vascular language prior to our

breathed language, corporeal, chemical,
drawing our sound into its harmonic, tuning
us to what we've not yet seen, the surround
calling us, theory-less, toward an inference
of horizontal connections there at

ground level, an incantation in-
dependent (of us) but detectable, **consummate**
always resistant (to us) but inciting
our recognition of what it might mean
to be **here**—among others human and not—

here, home, where ours is another of the small
voices taking us over, over ourselves
over into the **nothing-between**, the out
of sight of ourselves, a litany from
spore-bearing mouths as

hyphae stretch their **long** necks
and open their throats opening
a link between systems
a supersaturation of syntax
an **arousal** even as slow-

rolling walls of high-decibel
sonar blow out the **ears** of whales and
fires burn uncontrolled and
slurry pits leak into the creek, etc.
etc., femicides, war, righteous

insistence and still
and **still** the lived sensation fits
into the living sensorium, can't
you hear—*Don't be so
rational*—the world **inhale**?—hear

the call from elsewhere which
is just where we are, no, even
closer, **inside** us inside the blood-
pulse of our bodies, the bristle of
our mosses, the **embrace**—, and exhale

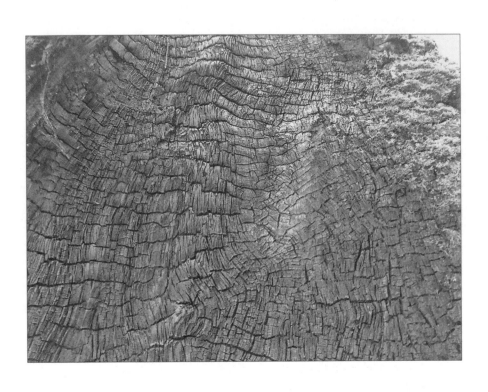

THE REDWOODS

• • •

—while nearby, but where?

/ \

in that terpenated air among   iterated redwood limbs

\   / \

now flocked   with mats of epiphyte,

/ |

/   a Steller's jay starts and restarts

/   /

its shredded arpeggios—   *not description* —and

\   \

one of a nesting murrelet's soft   black eyes mirrors

/

the harlequinades of a vole,　　　　plump, whiskered

　　\　　　　　　　　　　　　　　　　　|

　　cylinder of fur diligently—*this is*　　　*not description but an un-*

　　　\　　　　　　　　　　　　　　　/

　　　acknowledged chapter—　　　stuffing its cheeks

　　　　/

　　with green needles

while two hundred feet below,   in the understory,

/   /

whipplevine punctured by   snags and deadfall and sorrel

| /

and sword and bracken fern   splashing up from the soil—*not*

\\   \\

description but an un-   *acknowledged chapter of our*

\\   /

own memoir—rich with   chumbling volcanics,

/   \\   /

andesite mostly, and dacite, and rotting redwood needles that

\\   /

lightly tremble with nematodes and some   /

                   spider like arthropod who can name?

\

a ground squirrel, crossing   the dry creek edged
/   \   —
with alder, its tail   vertical as a flagpole, *its*
/   \
instance, all instances   *interpenetrating,*
\   /
an endless memoir of   *ravelment in which our case*
\   \
likewise has been underwritten—
| /
careens between   its burrow and fire caves in
/   /
the massive redwood trunks   glistening with slug trails, rimmed
\ |
by rooting mushrooms

On the way to • to the site of his • cabin, his temple • refurbished

from the plundered • temple of another religion • a religion of

fishermen • on the Tokelalume aka • Lagunitas Creek in Devil's

• Gulch, the path into the forest flagged • flagged on either side

with orange • sticky monkey flowers • innumerable stubby,

macho • fence lizards rush in bursts • ahead of you like heralds

as • you come up the trail, but • half a mile in, a single • Western

skink, its neon-blue tail hauled upright behind it • races diagonally

crosstrail and disappears • beneath thimbleberry brambles mantled

• with shredded spiderweb

in the epic literature of India • which all those years ago • he was

reading, lying • on this greywacke slab • above the ebulliently

plashing • creek, his head in shade, his • lanky body warm • legs

crossed in the sun's • maple light breaking through • tree limbs

pajamaed in moss • and stretching awkwardly out • out over the

gulch • from a steep hillside held in place • only by radial green

explosions • of bracken, Maidenhair fern, and • a pair of red-

spiked black caterpillars • which crawl onto his leather boots • set

side by side in the rampant pipevine the • caterpillars have been
devouring • in all that epic literature of India • no more than three
colors • are mentioned

See? He is here and not here. Not • unlike you yourself. Or the
water • striders in the creek • rowing in punctuated contractions •
against the drift. What • you see in the clear absolute of the water
• as you stand on some paleostump at the bank • under an electric
insect whine • distributed perfectly throughout the canopy, • what
you see below • in the pellucid water is a cluster of • six Gothic
black shadowdots • cast onto the streambed • below the thin, sand-
colored • bodies of the actual water striders • who are bowed all
but invisibly above • the tensile surface of the stream

Not here. And here. And though you • you have hiked the dirt
path through the forest • as he did before you were born • to the
familiar place, the confluence • of two modest falls, to the ground
truth • the little clearing where he snored • and fried two eggs for
breakfast and sat • cross legged on a slab of rock scribbling • into

the future that holds you in it, • you are only still arriving • still

• arriving • no trace of the cabin left, and yet • his presence is

not • decomposable, your mind • merges with what is not • your

mind, your happiness • is radiant and you squat, listening • in the

tangible density of what is and isn't there • as you become your •

shadow fluidly contiguous • with the shadows of trees

SANGAM ACOUSTICS:
CONFLUENCE OF TIME, SPACE,
AND THE HUMAN SELF

BY N. MANU CHAKRAVARTHY

Forest, Pastoral, Sea, Mountain, Wasteland. The five primary landscapes of Sangam literature are also the definitive landscapes of California, my birthplace and home. My "Sangam Acoustics" are influenced by my own experiences in India and California and by translations of Sangam poems which allude to one of those five topographies. Because cultural influences are complicated matters, even when the original is to be celebrated, and because Sangam poetics are so little known in the United States, I've asked the literary scholar N. Manu Chakravarthy to provide some context for Sangam poetics. —F. G.

"Sangam" refers to a gathering of individuals united in spirit, sharing a common vision, and, in a metaphysical sense, seeking meaning and purpose in a state of togetherness. The element of conviviality guides and nourishes the community of seekers, though it needs to be stated without any ambiguity that the commonness of seeking does not erase differences and divergences among individuals who form such a community. Homogeneity and hierarchy are alien to a true Sangam. The particular and specific visions of different individuals only enhance the spirit of Sangam.

The expression Sangam is rooted in the Jaina and Buddhist religious / philosophical traditions, the essence of which is captured in the Buddhist prayer, "Buddham Sharanam Gacchami, Sangam Sharanam Gacchami,

N. *Manu Chakravarthy, the distinguished literary critic and winner of the National Film Award for Best Critic of the Year, is Professor of English at NMKRV College, Bengaluru. He has written extensively on literature, music, feminism, politics, and cinema.*

Dhammam Sharanam Gacchami"—meaning "I shall go to invoke the Buddha, embrace the Sangha, and follow the Dhamma." The prayer is indeed a declaration that one seeks the Buddha through the "sangha" and by adhering to the principles of the "Dhamma." The attainment of what is sought is deeply personal and, in a qualified sense, collective.

Classical Tamil literature has been recognized as "Sangam literature" and is acknowledged to have flourished between 300 B.C. and 300 A.D. Many claims have been advanced about the duration of the Sangam period, some so exaggerated they border on being mythological narratives. However, the term Sangam seems to have come to classical Tamil literature from Jaina and Buddhist sources.

Scholars recognize three Sangam periods and admit that texts belonging to the first Sangam do not appear to have survived. A text of grammar and rhetoric called "Tolkappiyam" is said to belong to the second Sangam, and the third Sangam comprises a wide range of lyrics on love that form an anthology called the "Kuruntokai." In accordance with thematic patterns, Tamil poems have been categorized as "Akam" and "Puram."

"Akam" poems are focused on an *inner realm*, while the "puram" ones refer to public spaces. Akam poems are essentially love poems and deal with the different existential/emotional states of the persona, whereas Puram poems are concerned with war, the glory of kings and heroes, and ethical values. Puram poetry has a historical/social context and is quite strongly grounded in the physical realities of the world. Akam poems are not, in the strict sense of the term, historical and are not realistic in a definable manner, which, however, does not mean that they have no sense of reality. Akam poetry is about the manner in which the realities of the world—and the elements of Nature—come fully alive in the experiential states of the persona/

personae of the poems. Nature—through flowers, mountains, birds, animals, barren lands, forests, seasons—corresponds with the "inner landscape" of the individual. Consequently, birds, beasts, and the elemental forces of nature are consciously shifted to "alien locations" far beyond their original habitat, registering and underlining the shifting moods of the persona. The translocation/dislocation of "the natural order of things" is quite unique to Sangam poetry. In other words, the "exterior" precisely relates to the one who beholds it—through varied emotions created by states of longing, craving, union, fulfillment, separation, infidelity, betrayal, and so on. Thus, "nature" is what the human mind makes of it. It is because of this that the specific identity of a natural object dramatically alters to register an altogether different identity and essence of experience related to the emotional state of the persona. The extraordinary crisscrossing of natural elements is a great marker of the strength of the *inner landscape* that human consciousness carries, transforming external nature to match its own form and temper. Furthermore, nature exists in its various forms with all basic qualities intact, but in Sangam poetry "nature" extends beyond itself to "become" a metaphor of the mind. The metamorphosis of nature in Sangam poetry is essentially an internalization of the *exterior landscape*, dissolving distinctions of opposition and separation between the self's intensity of experience and the so-called impassive spirit of physical reality. "Nature" is congruent with the human spirit.

Forrest Gander's "Sangam Acoustics" is, in the most exalted sense, the blossoming of the Sangam consciousness. Gander's poetry belongs to the Akam genre. Like the kurinchi flower (one of the most significant motifs of Sangam poetry) that blooms once in twelve years, Gander's "Sangam Acoustics" is Sangam resonating and illumining, in the Californian landscape, through Sea, Mountain, Pastoral, Forest, and

Wasteland, revealing for our times the organic relationship between the "experiencing human self" and the "phenomena of nature." Gander's poems unfold the Californian landscape and find expression in American dialect, but they cannot, by any stretch of imagination, be regarded as imitations, cultural incorporations or appropriations of the cultural ethos of Tamil Sangam. There is no act of transgression or violation of the sanctity of one realm by another, which in strict temporal terms is an alien entity. For that matter Gander's "Sangam Acoustics" cannot even be interpreted as an inspired attempt to *translate* the cultural idiom of classical Tamil into the modern American idiom.

Gander's "Sangam Acoustics" needs to be read as a spontaneous and deeply reflective *incarnation* of the "Sangam consciousness," constituted by its immutable spirit. If Tamil Sangam comes alive with its very well-defined and unique features of Tamil landscapes, "Sangam Acoustics" evokes the pulsating spirit of the Californian landscape. The uniqueness of each spatiotemporal realm is kept ethically intact. What is strikingly fascinating in Gander's poetry is that through the uniqueness of each realm, a "universal Sangam spirit" emerges, unfolding the metaphorical confluence of varied and diverse physical selves, states of being, and apparently incomparable landscapes. In a complex and sophisticated manner, Gander's poetry contests simplistic and reductionist binaries of East and West, Tamil and English. Gander's inclusive and all-encompassing visions, transcending oppressive hierarchies of space and time, have a timeless quality, moving the reader to see the personae of his poems having several incarnations, like the Bodhisattvas. The "timeless" state of the "Sangam spirit" seems to manifest itself like an epiphany in Gander's work. Invoking the mystic William Blake, it could be said that "Sangam Acoustics" attains a poetic progression through the contraries that constitute its edifice.

It is in the dense and rich confluence of Tamil and Californian Sangam, with all the multiple and divergent echoes, resonances, sounds, colors of each realm so consciously consecrated, that the word "acoustics" gathers new and fresh meaning. The sharp nuances, the subtle tones, and the deep colors of each landscape work to brilliantly uphold the universality of the human spirit that—though strongly bound to its physical world—strives to transcend crippling boundaries of time and space through the strength of concrete experiences and not through vague and amorphous ideas. The full recognition of the truth of physicality is indeed the moment of birth of a transcendental holistic "Sangam life spirit." Forrest Gander's "Sangam Acoustics" illustrates this in an exemplary way.

ACKNOWLEDGMENTS

I'm particularly grateful, for a number of reasons, to Lynn Keller. It was she who invited me to collaborate with her, with the mycologist Anne Pringle, and with the artist Emily Arthur at Huron Mountain Wildlife Foundation, an experience that birthed the "Twice Alive" series.

And to Karin Gander, all our lives together.

Thanks to my international poet-companions among the lichens: foremost, to Brenda Hillman. Also to Mats Söderlund, Julio de la Vega, Camillo Sbarbaro, Drew Milne, Devin Johnston, Whit Griffin, and Peter O'Leary, and to Lew Welch, who wrote of lichen: "These are the stamps on the final envelope." To Paul Stamets, Lynn Margulis, Anne Pringle, David Griffiths, Thomas H. Nash, and Jane Bennett.

And to New Directions, all souls there, but especially Declan Spring, Mieke Chew, and Brittany Dennison, who were so involved with this book. And to you Eliot "El Faro" Weinberger, Calvin Bedient, James Byrne, Arthur Sze, Don Mee Choi, Roberto Harrison, Cole Swensen, Robert Hass, Sharon Olds, Nancy Kuhl, Joan Retallack, John Keene, Laura Mullen, Richard Deming, Dan Beachy-Quick, Roberto Tejada, Monica de la Torre.

Brecht, without you, without C, not a lick of this, nothing at all.

"Twice Alive" is for Lynn Keller. "Twice Alive II" is for Brenda Hillman. "Post-fire Forest" is for Maya Khosla; "The Redwoods" is for my Aussie friend Stuart Cooke from whom I purloined the form. "Sea: Night Surfing in Bolinas" is for Stephen Ratcliffe.

Photographs in "The Redwoods" are by Forrest Gander.

Thanks to the editors of the magazines that published some of these poems:

"The Redwoods" was commissioned and published by *Emergence Magazine* as a collaboration with the artist Katie Holten (eds. Bethany Ritz and Emmanuel Vaughan-Lee).

"The Redwoods" appeared with my photographs in *Lana Turner: A Journal of Arts & Criticism* (ed. Calvin Bedient).

"Forest" appeared in *Scientific American* (ed. Dava Sobel).

"Rexroth's Cabin" appeared in *Conjunctions* (ed. Bradford Morrow).

"Immigrant Sea" and "Post-fire Forest" appeared in *Forfatternes klimaaksjon*, a Norwegian climate magazine (ed. Mats Söderlund).

"Immigrant Sea" appeared in Polish translation in *Przekrój* (ed. Julia Fiedorczuk).

Poetry videos of "Immigrant Sea" and "Forest" (as "Interior Landscape") appeared at *Big Other* (ed. John Madera).

"Pastoral" appeared in *Poetry Daily* (ed. Jane Hirshfield).

"In the Mountains" appeared in *Cordite* (ed. Jeet Thayil).

Sections of "Twice Alive" appeared in *Republic of Apples, Democracy of Oranges: New Eco-Poetry from China and the U.S.* (eds. Frank Stewart, Tony Barnstone, and Ming Di, University of Hawaii Press, 2019). Thanks to Ming Di.

"Aubade" appeared in *Together in a Sudden Strangeness: America's Poets Respond to the Pandemic* (ed. Alice Quinn, Alfred A. Knopf, 2020).

I'm grateful for translations and exegesis of Sangam literature by M. I. Thangappa, A. R. Venkatachalapathy, A. K. Ramanujan, and others, and for a fruitful friendship with N. Manu Chakravarthy.